Storybook Dolls

Storybook Dolls

Valerie Janitch
with photographs by Rob Matheson

FABER & FABER
London · Boston

First published in 1979
by Faber and Faber Limited
3 Queen Square London WC1
Set, printed and bound in Great Britain by
Fakenham Press Limited, Fakenham, Norfolk

Conditions of Sale

British Library Cataloguing in Publication Data

Janitch, Valerie
    Storybook dolls
    1. Dollmaking   2. Soft toy making   3. Doll
    clothes
    I. Title
    745.59'22   *TT175*

ISBN 0–571–11313–3
ISBN 0–571–11314–1 Pbk

Contents

Storybook Dolls *page* 9

Introducing – The Doll with So Many Roles to Play. . . . 11

Methods and Materials: I 13
Equipment : Adhesives : Measurements : Making Patterns (traced and scale) : Cutting Felt : Sewing Felt : Vilene or Pellon : Colours and Trimmings : Following the Directions

Methods and Materials: II 16
Shoes : Setting in Sleeves : Fitted Bodices : Finishing Touches

Begin with the Basic Figure 18

Hair and Hairstyles 25
Loose Hair : Styled Hair : The Basic Style

Queen Guinevere 28

Maid Marion 33

The Wicked Fairy at the Sleeping Beauty's Christening 36

Hans Andersen's 'Real Princess' 39

Titania – Queen of the Fairies 45

Little Miss Muffet 51

Snow White 56

Red Riding Hood 58

Cinderella 61

Mary-Mary, Quite Contrary 64

Lucy Locket, Lost her Pocket. . . . 68

Old Mother Hubbard (and her Dog) 73

Where to Buy the Materials 79

Storybook Dolls

Watching a pantomime or film presentation of a favourite fairytale or traditional story, the things I most enjoy are the imaginative settings and costumes.

Years ago, the heroine's dresses were always very romantic, extravagantly trimmed with frills and flowers and ribbons: as long as they looked glamorous, no-one bothered too much about basing them on real fashions from the past. But nowadays, stage, film and television produce much more realistic dramatisations, which are usually set in some specific period of history – and talented designers are employed to create beautiful costumes inspired by the fashions of that time. Perhaps you have noticed a similar trend in the illustrations for recent editions of nursery rhymes and fairytales: the characters are dressed in authentic historical costume – resulting in some lovely books in which the enchanting pictures are almost more captivating than the familiar rhymes and well-loved stories!

Using this idea, I have made a collection of dolls dressed as some of the favourite fictional characters of my childhood. I imagined each one in the costume of a suitable historical period, spanning the centuries from the Middle Ages to just over a hundred years ago.

I didn't want to waste time making a complicated doll: so I designed one that was very quick, with only the parts that show needing to be properly made and finished: what the eye doesn't see – doesn't matter! Nor did I want to be bothered with tiny hems and fiddly turnings and careful finishing . . . so I used felt and non-woven interfacing fabrics that don't fray: they are lovely to work with, and form an ideal ground for all kinds of exciting trimmings. The hair is knitting wool or yarn, with variations on a basic style creating different effects. The features are deliberately simple, too, needing no artistic ability or embroidery skill: all the expression is contained in the eyes – which are nothing more than circles of felt and straight stitches.

So, with all the tedious chores eliminated, one is left with the pleasure and satisfaction of adding those tiny details which make each doll's costume recognisably true to period, and emphasise the charm of the character it represents. I hope you will enjoy making these examples as much as I did. And then I hope you will use my designs as a basis to expand this collection to include *your* special favourites, too.

Introducing – The Doll with So Many Roles to Play. . . .

I want you to enjoy making these costume dolls. So to help you enjoy making them, I have either speeded up, or cut out completely, all the boring bits!

For instance, it's always fun to make a doll: but in this case, the really exciting part is dressing it . . . so you won't want to spend too much time on the doll. This one is such a cheat that I'm too ashamed to call it a doll – it's just a 'basic figure'. The parts that show – head, hands and feet – are felt, stuffed with Kapok or any similar soft filling (don't use foam chips). The rest of the body is formed from pipe cleaners (to make it very flexible) wrapped around with 1-cm (⅜-in) thick sheet foam, which is sold at Woolworth's and other stores for padding and cushioning ironing boards, table mats, etcetera. Oversew the foam with large stitches – as rough and uneven as you like, because no-one will see them!

The clothes are 'made on' to the doll – so you can forget all about fiddly fastenings and setting sleeves into bodices and so on. And this also ensures a superb fit, because the clothes can be stitched to the body to hold them securely in position – and bodices can be drawn tightly round to emphasise a tiny waist.

You couldn't hope to work with an easier material than felt. Firm but soft to cut and sew: no hems or awkward turnings: no troublesome 'direction' or 'one way', as with woven fabrics (which makes it very economical, too). And the lovely colours inspire you-the-artist to plan dramatic colour schemes: try combining subtle shades – then experiment with vibrant contrasts.

Finally, to emphasise the quick-and-easy theme, you'll find a tube of fabric adhesive is a much neater and more efficient way to fix braids and trimmings, than lots of tedious sewing!

I have tried to avoid delaying you with pages of preliminary theory: I'm all for practical experience wherever possible. There are a few general directions which will help you get the best results from the patterns and instructions which follow. It is worth checking through these before you begin, because it will save time later on. Make a mental note of the points in Section I. But just glance through Section II at this stage: you can return to study these specific items in detail when you come to do the different operations described.

Methods and Materials: I

Equipment

No special tools are necessary – just your usual sewing things. The most important items are efficient scissors and plenty of sharp, medium-fine needles. And to be really professional, have an old-fashioned block of beeswax: drawing your thread through it before sewing prevents knotting and breaking.

Adhesives

Use a latex (or rubber solution) for all fabrics, paper, etcetera: my own choice is Copydex – which comes in a tube, with a useful little spatula. You will occasionally need a special all-purpose clear adhesive for non-porous surfaces, like glass beads, sequins and so on: Bostik Stik n'fix is ideal, and easier to use than some other types. American readers will find Sobo an excellent alternative to both of these glues.

Measurements

Both Imperial and metric measures are given in every case. Use one or the other – but don't compare the two: If you do, you will find they differ! This is because I have always given the nearest *practical* measurement, rather than an accurate conversion.

For instance, on the same dress I might use 1-cm wide ribbon and 1-cm wide lace; however, if you are using Imperial measurements, a narrower ribbon might look better – whilst the lace could be improved by being wider. So for your version, the ribbon would be interpreted as $\frac{1}{4}$ in wide, whilst the lace would be $\frac{1}{2}$ in. On the other hand, it would be ridiculous to tell metricated readers they need 6.5-mm wide ribbon and 12.5-mm wide lace!

So just use the ruler you prefer: measuring is equally clear on both. And either way, you can be sure the result will be perfectly in proportion.

Making Patterns

TO TRACE PATTERNS: Use household greaseproof paper (unwaxed parchment-type kitchen paper) or good quality white tissue paper – and a sharp pencil. When a fold is indicated, always *fold the paper*: run your thumbnail along to sharpen the crease, then place it exactly level with the fold-line on the pattern. Trace through the double thickness and then cut out, holding tightly or pinning to ensure the paper stays exactly together as you cut, so that when you open it out the two halves of the pattern are identical.

SCALE PATTERNS: Use graph paper – or draw the diagrams to the correct scale on tracing paper (as above) fixed firmly over a sheet of graph or squared paper. Use a sharp pencil and ruler, and compasses.

Cutting Felt

Use small, pointed scissors: make sure they are well-aligned and really sharp. Always cut the felt flat, not folded, and never cut a double thickness when working with tiny pieces and detailed shapes. When you need the same shape more than once, cut the first piece in single felt, using your paper pattern: then use this felt shape as your pattern for subsequent pieces – cutting the edges absolutely level.

Sewing Felt

Unless otherwise instructed, always oversew seams: an allowance of 1.5 mm ($\frac{1}{16}$ in) is made on all pattern pieces. Right sides together, pin or tack (baste) the two edges, exactly level, and join, oversewing with small, neat stitches in matching thread – close together and about 1.5 mm ($\frac{1}{16}$ in) deep. Turn to the right side and press the seam open with your thumbnail.

Vilene or Pellon

This firm, non-woven interfacing material comes in a variety of weights – all of them in white, and some in black. It is used as a stiff lining or separate petticoat under many of the dresses, but I have also used lighter weights for sleeves, collars, fichus, veils, etcetera. If you haven't any Vilene (U.K.) or Pellon (U.S.), use the most suitable substitute you have for that particular purpose. If felt nor net won't do, try to find a woven fabric that doesn't fray too easily – cotton or lawn are better than silky

14

materials: draw a few threads along straight cut edges if you don't want to make a hem, or you can seal them with a touch of fabric adhesive.

Colours and Trimmings

You will, of course, want to choose and plan your own colour schemes – and not necessarily follow my suggestions. However, to make the directions clear and easy to follow, I have identified the parts of each costume by the colours shown in the photographs. The same rule applies to trimmings and decoration: I have described the item I have used in each case – although you may wish to substitute something quite different.

Following the Directions

It is important to do each operation in the correct order. So be sure to follow the directions exactly as they are set out – otherwise you may find yourself in difficulties!

Methods and Materials: II

Shoes

Plan the footwear to suit the costume, matching or contrasting the colours as you please. Make the shoes from ribbon – embroidered is especially pretty, velvet and satin are very smart, for dainty pumps – or use braid or lace, or just narrow strips of matching felt. Whatever you choose, don't have it narrower than 5 mm ($\frac{1}{4}$ in) or wider than 1 cm ($\frac{3}{8}$ in). Add a bead, button, tiny lace or artificial flower, ribbon bow or other trimming to a plain toe: a silver sequin makes a smart buckle.

Soles should be brown or black.

Setting in Sleeves

Non-fray fabrics, and the fact that the sleeves are always 'made on' the doll, mean you avoid all the tricky problems of setting sleeves into armholes. Individual sleeve directions are given for each design, but as a general rule for a perfect result, set-in sleeves should be fitted as follows.

Join the side seam and turn to the right side, trimming lower edge, etcetera, if instructed. Gather close to top edge, beginning and ending at the seam. Fit sleeve over arm, draw up gathers round top, centre of sleeve matched to shoulder seam and side seam underneath – gathers distributed evenly, with a little more fullness around the top. Then drive your needle up into the armpit and out through the top of the arm, level with the shoulder seam – so that the top of the sleeve seam is caught under the arm, and the top of the sleeve secured to the shoulder. Catch edge of sleeve over edge of flesh felt all round. Fit bodice as directed. and slip-stitch armhole edges neatly over tops of sleeves.

Fitted Bodices

It is essential to trace the bodice patterns and cut your felt especially carefully, to ensure the shape is accurate. This is so important because all the shaping of the doll's figure is in the *dress* – not the body. Her 'vital

16

statistics' are contained in the bodice – like an old-fashioned stiff corset, which was made to the shape the wearer wished to be – and was then laced tightly round her so that she fitted it, rather than it fitting her! So make sure you cut the curves just as the pattern shows. Make neat seams, oversewing the edges with small stitches close together: turn to the right side and press the seam flat with your thumbnail. Try on the doll to check: adjust the shoulders if necessary, snipping away a little felt to give a really close, smooth fit.

Then you can be quite certain that when you sew the bodice round the foam, your doll's figure will go in and out beautifully in all the right places!

Finishing Touches

Look out for anything tiny in the way of odd beads, diamanté or rhinestone 'jewels' and so on, for decoration: broken necklaces, odd ear-rings and old brooches are a good source of jewellery. Or you can buy little boxes of tiny coloured beads or seed pearls in several sizes.

Narrow fancy braids are often needed to edge a hem or decorate a bodice or headdress: find these in the lampshade or dress trimmings department. Incidentally, a narrow braid can sometimes be cut in half down the centre to make it half the width!

Always buy the narrowest lace and ribbon available – unless otherwise specified.

opposite: Snow White
previous page: Lucy Locket

Begin with the Basic Figure

MATERIALS: Flesh or deep cream felt, 18 cm (7 in) square, for head and hands

Beige, putty, flesh or coloured felt, 10 cm (4 in) square, for feet

Scrap of brown or black felt for soles

Scrap of black felt for eyes

20 cm (8 in) ribbon, braid, felt, etcetera, for shoes (see SHOES – p. 16)

Sheet foam, 20 cm (8 in) square × 1 cm ($\frac{3}{8}$ in) thick, for the body

Kapok, polyester fiberfill or similar soft stuffing

Eight pipe cleaners

Black sewing thread for eyes

Thin stiff card for soles

Adhesive tape (optional)

Fabric adhesive

CUT IN FELT: 1 head front

1 head back

4 hands (see below – 4)

2 feet

2 soles

CUT IN FOAM: 1 arms

1 body

2 legs

1. Arms

Overlap two pipe cleaners to measure 24 cm (9½ in) in all. Join by taping ends as indicated (or bind with thread), leaving centre free.

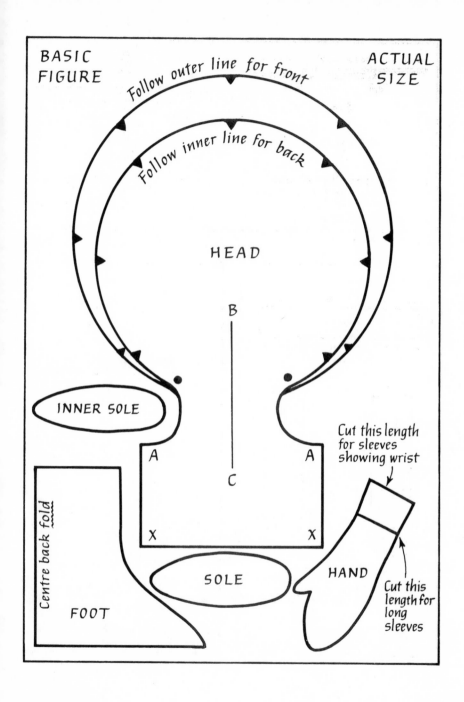

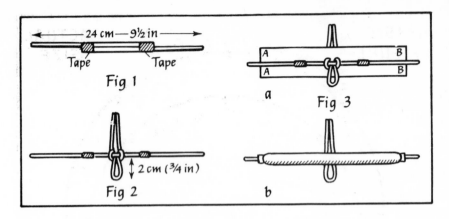

Fig 1 — 24 cm—9½ in — Tape — Tape

Fig 2 — 2 cm (¾ in)

Fig 3 — a — A B — A B — b

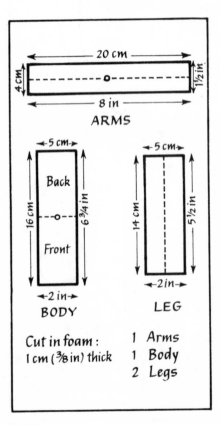

ARMS — 20 cm — 8 in — 4 cm — 1½ in

BODY — 5 cm — Back — Front — 16 cm — 6¾ in — 2 in

LEG — 5 cm — 14 cm — 5½ in — 2 in

Cut in foam: 1 Arms
1 cm (⅜ in) thick 1 Body
  2 Legs

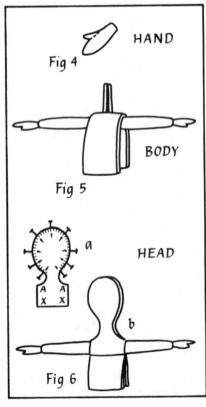

Fig 4 — HAND

Fig 5 — BODY

HEAD — a — A A — X X — b

Fig 6

2. Bend another pipe cleaner in half and push both ends up between the double section at centre of arms, leaving bent middle 2 cm (¾ in) below; then twist each end round arms once, and leave pointing up for the neck.

3. Place on foam – protruding 2 cm (¾ in) at each end: push neck pipe cleaner through hole in centre of foam, then fold foam in half round the pipe cleaners, and oversew edges A–B: wrap thread tightly round ends of foam to form wrists.

4. Hands
Cut twice in flesh felt: I gave my dolls little thumbs, but if you think they are a bit fiddly to cut out, just cut as the broken line, and ignore them. Cut each piece a second time, using the first felt shape as a pattern: leave pinned together. Making very tiny stitches, oversew neatly round the edge, leaving the wrist end open. Stuff lightly, then push a knitting needle through the stuffing to the tip of the fingers: withdraw needle and push pipe cleaner at end of arm well down into hole, catching wrist edge securely to foam (thumbs forward).

4a. To add wrist or forearm
Some dolls have sleeves that are not quite full-length. In these cases, cut a longer hand, to include the wrist, as indicated on the pattern. Make up, and fit, as above – but before making up the arms, cut the foam 1 cm (⅜ in) shorter at each end: push the pipe cleaner well down into the hand, as before.

5. Body
Fold in half as broken line: place arms inside fold, pushing neck up through centre hole.

6. Head
Run a gathering thread all round the outer edge of the *front*, between the dots. Pin front to back, matching circles and notches: draw up gathers to fit, distributing them evenly between the pins. Oversew together all round, continuing down to end of each shoulder (A), sewing round the neck very carefully: turn at A and *stitch back again* to dot.

Easing the felt gently through, a little at a time, turn to the right side. If you find this is stretching the neck too much, or is too difficult, flatten the head again – then cut a slit in the *back* as B–C: turn, then slip-stitch the edges neatly together again.

21

Stuff very firmly, moulding the head into a smoothly rounded shape, ending at base of neck. Make a central hole with a knitting needle as in hand, then push neck pipe cleaner well up into head, so the folded body foam fits close under shoulder seams. Catch front and back securely together at X's, under each arm.

7. *Legs*

Put two pipe cleaners together and oversew leg foam round, level with pipe cleaners at the bottom – excess protruding at the top. Draw up lower edge tightly, as arms.

Hook exposed pipe cleaners at top through loop under arms, and bend ends down to secure.

Bend another pipe cleaner in half. Push the bent end up inside the

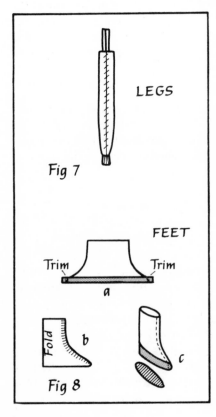

LEGS

Fig 7

FEET

Trim   Trim

a

Fold b

c

Fig 8

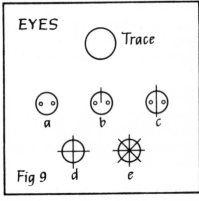

EYES

Trace

a   b   c

Fig 9   d   e

body, behind the arms, into the neck. Then push each separate end into the top of a leg.

Finally, catch sides of body together at the natural waistline, and bind twice with thread.

8. Feet

Stick ribbon, etcetera, level with lower edge, as indicated: trim ends. Right side inside, fold in half and oversew front edge. Turn to right side.

Cut the inner sole in card and stick to inside of sole. Matching toes and centre back of heel, oversew the lower edge of the foot neatly round the sole.

Stuff to halfway up ankle. Push base of leg down inside, and catch top edge of felt neatly to foam.

Trim shoes as required (see SHOES – p. 16).

8a. Boots

Make the *whole foot* in black – or the colour of your choice – omitting the strip for the shoe. Sew tiny beads at 5 mm intervals down the side of each boot, for buttons: I use seed pearls – either leaving them as pearl buttons, or colouring them to match the boot with a permanent marker or paint.

9. Eyes

Don't add the eyes until the doll is dressed – and never before doing the hair. Study their position carefully, making sure they are evenly spaced, and correctly balanced about halfway down the face: consult the illustrations for guidance.

Cut circles of black felt as shown. For an easy way to mark accurate circles on felt, find a cap from a pen or toothpaste tube, a tiny bottle top – or any similar round object with a firm rim – the same size as the required circle. Rub a white or light-coloured wax crayon or chalk all round the rim, then press it down firmly on your felt – and twist, taking care not to move the position. This should leave a clear impression on the felt: cut carefully round the marked line.

Place the eyes on the face to determine the best position, as described above. When you are satisfied, secure each with two pins, as diagram a.

Using black sewing thread, push your needle into the side of the face (under the hair or headdress), and come up in the centre of the eye. Make a straight stitch, as diagram b: then come up again in the centre – and make a second stitch, as diagram c. Remove the pins. Continue to make similar stitches, as diagrams d and e. When you have completed the eight stitches – *go over each one again*, then finish off at the side, as before. To avoid going round a second time, you can use double thread – but making a second stitch over the first allows you to lengthen any which are a little short.

Hair and Hairstyles

Make and dress your doll before adding the hair. The directions for each doll tell you when to do the hairstyle: at that stage, turn back to this section for all the basic information you need.

The method is always the same: wool or yarn is wound evenly round a piece of card, and then tied to form bunches of loops which are sewn and stuck to the head. The depth of the card is measured according to the length of hair required. The number of times the 'hair' is wound around the card is determined partly by the hairstyle – but mainly by the thickness of the wool or yarn. In each case, directions are given for the kind of wool or yarn which was used for the individual doll concerned – and you can see the effect in the photograph. However, if you want to substitute a thicker or thinner alternative, follow the directions, but adjust the number of times you wind the wool or yarn around the card accordingly: fewer times for a thicker wool – more for a thin one.

Loose Hair

Cut fairly stiff card about 10 cm (4 in) wide by the depth stated in the directions (a). Wind your wool or yarn evenly round it, the correct number of times (b). Then slip a single strand under the wool, against the card (c), and tie the loops together at one edge (d). Slide the loops off the card (e) and stitch the tied section to the head at the point directed.

When all the bunches of wool are in position, cut the loops at the bottom, and trim evenly to length all round. Stick the underneath hair lightly to the head wherever necessary.

Styled Hair

Prepare card, wind wool around it and tie as diagrams a–d: but before sliding off card, tie the loops at *both* edges (f). Then remove card and tie skein at the centre, tightly or loosely, as instructed: trim loose ends neatly (g).

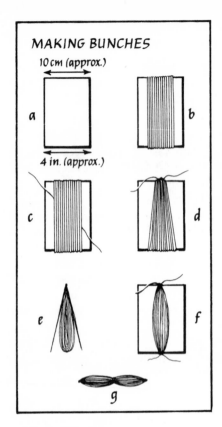

MAKING BUNCHES

10 cm (approx.)

a

b

4 in. (approx.)

c

d

e

f

g

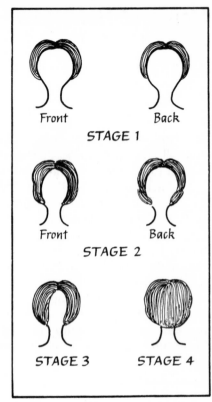

Front   Back

STAGE 1

Front   Back

STAGE 2

STAGE 3   STAGE 4

The Basic Style

This style, using double knitting wool or thick-knit yarn, is used for the majority of dolls in the book – with variations which are described in the individual directions. Remember that the finished effect of a style is almost entirely determined by the position of the front skein of hair (stage 2): it can be swept off the forehead – drawn right down over the face – or curved round somewhere between. Always follow the appropriate illustration for guidance.

Make tied skeins for styled hair, as above:

STAGE 1: Wind double knitting wool or thick-knit yarn twenty times around a 14-cm (5½-in) deep card: tie sides tightly, and centre fairly

26

tightly. Stick across top of head over seam: catch ends down securely.

STAGE 2: Wind wool ten times around a 17-cm (6¾-in) deep card. Tie as before. Stick in front of first piece, taking ends round to cover previous ends, and catching down just behind seam.

STAGE 3: Wind wool ten times around a 15-cm (6-in) deep card: tie sides and centre tightly. Stick centre close behind first piece: bring sides down over back of head, and catch over ends of second (front) skein.

STAGE 4: Wind wool ten times around a 13-cm (5-in) deep card: tie as last skein. Fold in half and stick centre immediately behind last piece, bringing ends down to cover rest of head, and catching neatly into place.

Queen Guinevere

In fact, King Arthur ruled in the sixth century. But he became a national hero only when the story of his legendary deeds in Camelot was written in the twelfth century. And that is the period of his queen's high-waisted gown and medieval wimple – with a golden crown and regal train to mark her royal status. As clothes at this time were basically still very simple, Guinevere's costume is particularly easy to make – just look at the pattern shapes!

MATERIALS: Lime felt, 20 cm (8 in) square, for skirt, and a scrap for cuffs
Lilac felt, 11 cm×20 cm (4¼ in×8 in), for bodice and hem
Purple felt, 20 cm×30–35 cm (8 in×12–14 in), for cloak
White felt for wimple and to trim cloak
Light-weight white Vilene or Pellon, 20 cm (8 in) square, for veil
Very thin card (or cartridge – or construction – paper) for crown and belt
Metallic gold paper (or gold paint) for crown
12 cm (4½ in) decorative braid, 1.5 cm (⅝ in) wide, for belt
Very narrow gold braid to trim hem, cuffs, crown and cloak, as required (approximately 80 cm (30 in) as shown)
Additional fancy braids to decorate hem
Two tiny gold buttons for cloak
Sticky-both-sides tape (optional)
All-purpose clear adhesive (for gold foil paper)
Fabric adhesive

SKIRT: Fold the lime felt in half and oversew the two long edges to form centre back seam. Turn to right side.

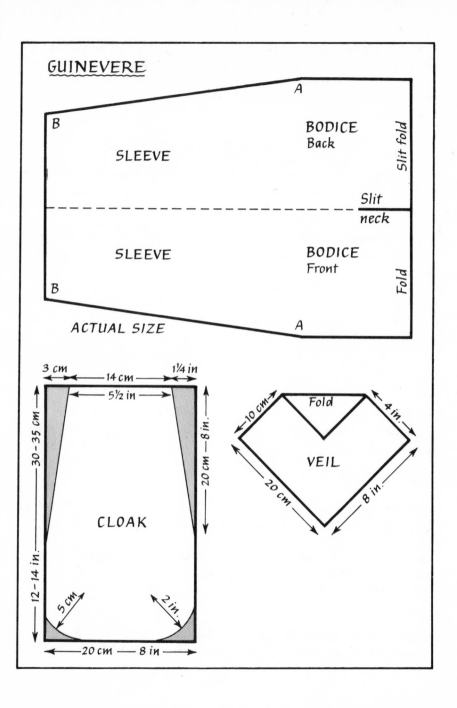

GUINEVERE

SLEEVE

BODICE
Back

Slit fold

B

Slit
neck

SLEEVE

BODICE
Front

Fold

B

ACTUAL SIZE

A

A

CLOAK

3 cm
14 cm
1¼ in
5½ in
30 – 35 cm
20 cm — 8 in.
12 – 14 in.
5 cm
2 in.
20 cm — 8 in

VEIL

10 cm
Fold
4 in.
20 cm
8 in.

Mark top edge into four. Gather close to edge: then make another line of gathers 1 cm ($\frac{3}{8}$ in) below the first. Fit skirt on doll and draw up gathers close under the arms, above the natural waist, distributing them evenly and catching securely to the body to hold in position.

Cut hem to length.

BODICE: Cut in lilac felt. Fold along broken line, and join sleeve seams between A–B. Turn to right side.

Fit bodice on doll. Make sure neck sits smoothly, then slip-stitch centre back seam. Stitch lower edges A–A neatly over skirt gathers.

Gather wrists and draw up tightly.

BELT: Cut a strip of thin card 1.5 cm × 12 cm ($\frac{1}{2}$ in × 5 in). Stick fancy braid over it, or decorate with jewels. Fit around waist, overlapping join at back.

HEM: Cut a strip of lilac felt 4 cm × 20 cm (1$\frac{1}{2}$ in × 8 in). Stick rows of trimming to form decoration, edging with narrow gold braid. Stick round skirt.

CUFFS: Cut 1.5-cm ($\frac{1}{2}$-in) wide strips of lime felt, and stitch round wrists. Edge with gold braid.

WIMPLE: Cut in white felt. Fit hole over face and wrap lower edge smoothly around neck, taking the corners up and overlapping o's at back of head: stitch securely. Pin x to top of head, then gather each edge between o–x: draw up tightly, and finally catch gathered edges together up back of head.

VEIL: Fold one corner of the Vilene or Pellon under, as diagram: then drape over head as illustrated, pinning to hold in place.

CROWN: Cut in card or paper, and cover both sides with gold foil paper. Stick overlap and fit on head, fixing with pins. Stick braid round lower edge, over pins. Adjust veil and hold in place with sticky-both-sides tape or dabs of adhesive.

CLOAK: Following the diagram, trim the sides, and round off the lower corners of your purple felt. Cut long strips of white felt 2.5 cm (1 in) wide.

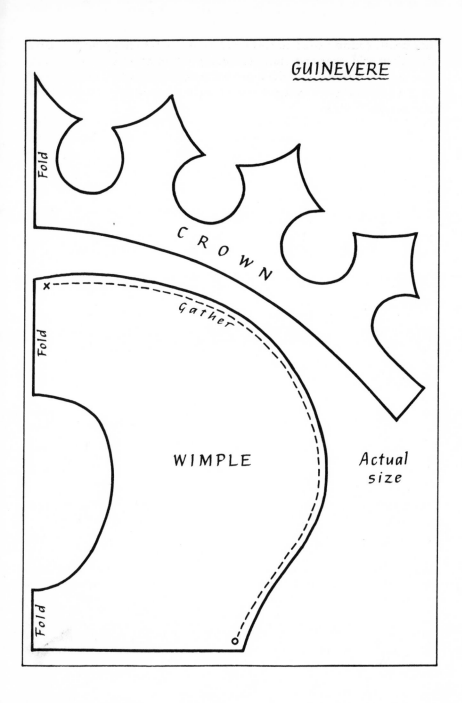

GUINEVERE

Fold

CROWN

Fold

Gather

WIMPLE

Fold

Actual
size

Stick neatly round sides and bottom of cloak, half overlapping the purple edge: then fold over and stick remaining half to other side of cloak.

Gather the top edge and draw up to fit around shoulders, as illustrated. Stitch a button at each top corner, then fix in position with a band of gold braid across the front.

opposite: Queen Guinevere
following page: Maid Marion

Maid Marion

Robin Hood's beautiful Maid Marion slips through Sherwood Forest to meet her lover. Green leaves under a clear sky are reflected in the soft colours of her medieval gown – with just a simple wreath of flowers to hold her flowing hair. To decide a subtle blending of colours for your Maid Marion, think of nature – woods, flowers, and the seasons . . . then choose from the shades which these suggest.

MATERIALS: Olive green felt, 30 cm (12 in) square, for dress
Pale blue felt, 15 cm × 18 cm (6 in × 7 in), for dress
Heavy Vilene or Pellon, 28 cm × 23 cm (11 in × 9 in), for petticoat
60 cm (⅝ yd) very narrow pale olive braid to trim sleeves
18 cm (7 in) blue and green embroidered flower trimming for neck
23 cm (9 in) pale blue sequins for belt
Tiny blue artificial flowers for headdress
Medium-weight wool or yarn for hair
Fabric adhesive

Cut the bodice front once, tracing pattern with centre fold: cut the back twice, following the broken line. Cut the sleeve twice, and the main skirt panel (a) four times, all in green.

Cut the under-sleeve twice, and the narrow skirt panel (b) four times, in blue.

UNDER-SLEEVE: Wrap tightly round arm, lower edge level with wrist, and slip-stitch overlap.

SLEEVE: Oversew side seam from o to x. Turn to right side. Gather close to top edge. Fit sleeve on arm, o on top, meeting shoulder seam. Draw up evenly around top of arm and stitch to edge of flesh felt.

33

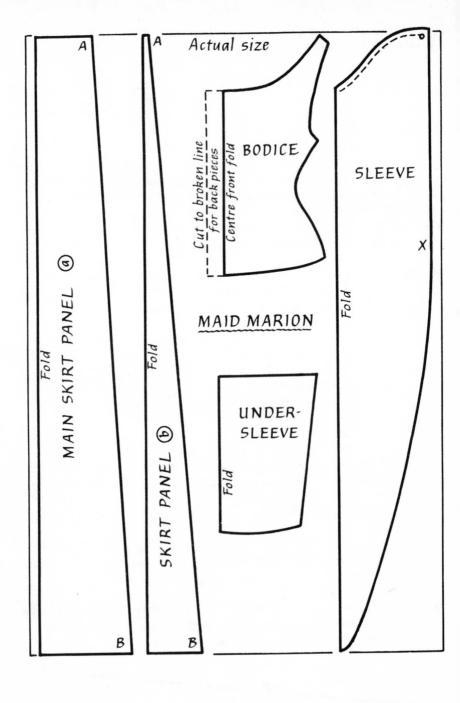

A

Actual size

Fold

MAIN SKIRT PANEL ⓐ

B

A

Fold

SKIRT PANEL ⓑ

B

Cut to broken line for back pieces

Centre front fold

BODICE

MAID MARION

UNDER-SLEEVE

Fold

SLEEVE

Fold

X

BODICE: Oversew the front to the two back pieces along sides and at shoulders. Turn to right side. Overlap centre back edges and join at base.

SKIRT: Right sides together, oversew green and blue panels together alternately, between A–B. When all eight pieces are joined, press the seams open and pin the flat piece on to the Vilene or Pellon. Cut this level with the edge of the felt – for the petticoat. Un-pin, then make final seam joining skirt panels.

Gather round top edge. Then, right sides together, pin evenly round lower edge of bodice, with a wide panel (a) at centre front, back and sides: draw up gathers to fit and oversew neatly together.

PETTICOAT: Join side edges to form centre back seam: stitch top edge over top edge of skirt. Turn dress to right side.

Fit dress on doll. Pin bodice overlap at centre back to fit smoothly. Slip-stitch armholes round tops of sleeves, then join bodice back.

TRIMMING: Fold sleeves back at x, and catch at each side to form a cuff, as illustrated. Stick narrow braid around edge. Stick sequins over waist join, one end hanging down at the front. Stick embroidered flower trimming around neck.

HAIR: Using medium-weight wool or yarn, make bunches of loops as directed for loose hair on p. 25 (diagrams a–e):

Sides: Make two bunches, winding wool twenty times around an 11-cm (4½-in) deep card for each. Tie tightly and stitch one at each side of head, over the seam (just above centre notch).
Back: Wind wool thirty times around a 14-cm (5½-in) deep card: tie tightly and stitch to back of head, at centre top, just behind the seam.
Top: Wind wool sixty times around a 16-cm (6½-in) deep card: tie *loosely*, then spread tied section across top of head, bringing down smoothly over sides and round to the back. Stitch and stick into place, cutting loops and trimming to length.

HEADDRESS: Bind single stems of flowers together to form one 'stalk' fitting halfway round the head: make a similar stalk and bind together to join at back. Pin around head as illustrated.

The Wicked Fairy at the Sleeping Beauty's Christening

Use a light beige or putty-coloured felt for the doll, to make the Bad Fairy look rather sinister and emphasise her evil character.

Choose dark, dramatic colours for her costume, too. Instead of purples – shades of brown, or deep blue, would look just as effective teamed with black, white and grey, as illustrated. Find all the dark, glittery trimmings you can, to decorate her dress: shimmering sequins, shiny black lace and tiny jet beads were just some of the treasures I unearthed! And I used narrow black lace (as that edging the cape) to give her very dainty fairy shoes.

MATERIALS: Plum felt, 19 cm×21 cm (7½ in×8½ in), for skirt
Lavender felt, 10 cm×21 cm (4 in×8½ in), for skirt
Grey felt, 8 cm×20 cm (3 in×8 in), for bodice
Heavy Vilene or Pellon, 31 cm×26 cm (12 in×10 in), to line skirt
Medium-weight soft white Vilene or Pellon (or felt), 16 cm×11 cm (6½ in×4½ in), for wimple
Transparent white Vilene or Pellon (or fine net or chiffon), 14 cm (5½ in) square, for veil
Medium-weight black Vilene or Pellon (or felt), 25 cm×35 cm (10 in×14 in), for headdress and cape
25 cm (¼ yd) heavy black lace, 2.5 cm (1 in) wide, for headdress
1 metre (1 yd) narrow black lace to edge cape
60 cm (¾ yd) fancy braid, 1.5 cm (¾ in) wide, to trim hem, sleeves and waist
Lace, sequins, etcetera, to trim front panel of skirt
Tiny black beads
Toothpick, fancy sequins and diamanté or rhinestones, for wand

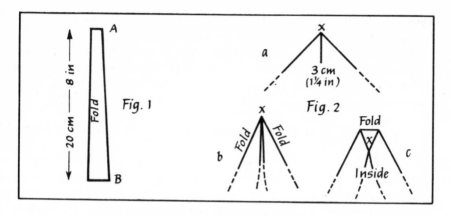

All-purpose clear adhesive (for wand)
Fabric adhesive

SKIRT: Trace the two skirt panels for Maid Marion (p. 34) *but lengthen them* (see diagram 1). To do this, mark 20 cm (8 in) on the centre fold of your tracing paper: trace the top and bottom lines to correspond with the marks, then join A–B. Cut the main panel (a) four times in plum, and the narrow panel (b) four times in lavender.

Right sides together, oversew the panels together alternately, between A–B. When all eight pieces are joined, press the seams open and tack (baste) the flat piece on to the Vilene or Pellon: cut this level with the edge of the felt. Make the final seam to join the skirt panels – avoiding the lining. Then join the straight edges of the lining, making a separate seam. Turn to right side.

Decorate one narrow panel, and edge with lace, sequins, etcetera, for the centre front. Stick or sew braid round the hem. Then gather the top edge (including lining), fit skirt on doll, narrow panels at centre front, back and sides, and draw up evenly – close under the arms, catching securely to the body to hold in position.

BODICE: Use the pattern for Guinevere (p. 29). Cut in grey felt: make up and fit as directed. Trim wrists and waistline with braid, as illustrated. Catch strings of tiny beads across the front, between shoulders.

WIMPLE: Use the pattern for Guinevere (p. 31). Cut in soft white Vilene or Pellon: make up and fit as directed.

STEEPLE HEADDRESS: Cut a 24-cm (9½-in) diameter semi-circle of black Vilene or Pellon. Twist round into a cone of double thickness, so that the two straight edges are level, one inside and one outside: stick join. Fit on doll, pinning and catching the lower edge to the head (join at back). Catch a loop of tiny black beads at centre front, over forehead. Stick wide black lace to overlap lower edge – raising it across the front, as shown.

VEIL: Catch one corner to tip of steeple: then catch the two corners below to back of head.

CAPE: Cut a 22-cm (8½-in) square of black Vilene or Pellon. Mark a 3-cm (1¼-in) diagonal line at one corner (diagram 2a): then fold the edges in to meet, level with it (diagram 2b). Now fold the corner down – 3 cm (1¼ in) below the tip (diagram 2c).

Edge with narrow lace, then stitch fold across back of shoulders (corner folded down inside).

WAND: Darken toothpick with ink or marker, then stick flower sequins, or alternative, back-to-back at the tip: finish with a glittering diamanté or rhinestone in the centre. Stitch to hand.

Hans Andersen's 'Real Princess'

The fairytale 'real princess' proved her royal blood by complaining that she could feel a pea under twenty mattresses. Personally, I've always thought her rather a snob – and *extremely* rude! However, it makes a romantic story, and they all lived happily ever after. So here is my version of Hans Andersen's princess. Her sixteenth-century costume is based on a real one worn by a *real* princess: Princess Elizabeth, before she became Queen Elizabeth I of England.

MATERIALS: Rose felt, 40 cm×33 cm (16 in×13 in), for dress
Coffee brown felt, 19 cm×12 cm (7½ in×5 in), for kirtle and sleeves
Black felt, 12 cm×16 cm (4½ in×6½ in), for hood
Heavy Vilene or Pellon interfacing, 33 cm×25 cm (13 in×10 in), for kirtle
110 cm (1¼ yd) narrow metallic braid or alternative to pattern kirtle
25 cm (10 in) narrow white lace
85 cm (1 yd) narrow cream braid, for under-sleeves
50 cm (20 in) cream braid, 1 cm (⅜ in) wide, to edge headdress
30 cm (12 in) narrow cream braid (above cut in half), to edge skirt
1 metre (1⅛ yd) narrow matching rose braid, for dress and headdress
115 cm (1½ yd) fancy coffee braid, to trim dress
25-cm (10-in) length of pearls, for headdress (optional)
Tiny gilt beads, ruby diamanté or rhinestone, large gold sequin, etcetera, for jewellery – or alternatives

39

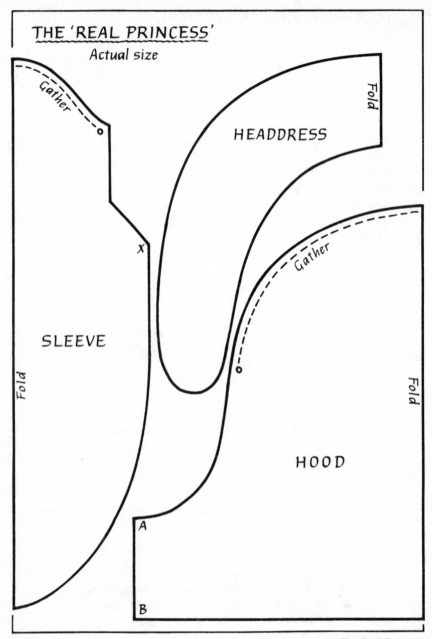

THE 'REAL PRINCESS'

Actual size

Gather

HEADDRESS

Fold

X

SLEEVE

Fold

Gather

Fold

HOOD

A

B

opposite: The Real Princess
following page: The Wicked Fairy

Thin card for headdress
Cartridge or construction paper for foundation
Face tissue
Double knitting wool or thick-knit yarn for hair
Fabric adhesive

SKIRT PATTERN: Follow diagram 1: centre A, draw a 42-cm (16½-in) diameter semi-circle, with a 6-cm (2⅜-in) semi-circle inside. Mark point C 18 cm (7 in) from B: then join A–C. Cut out, cutting away the shaded section.

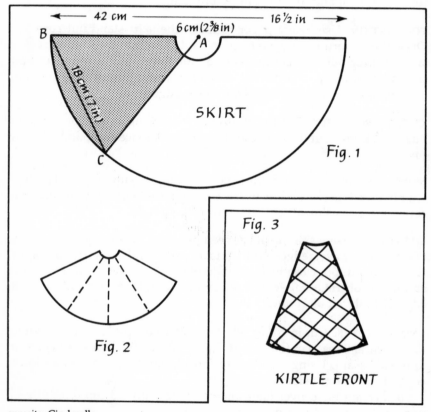

Fig. 1

SKIRT

Fig. 2

Fig. 3

KIRTLE FRONT

opposite: Cinderella
previous page: Little Red Riding Hood

KIRTLE: Cut skirt pattern in heavy interfacing.

Now mark the pattern equally into four (diagram 2). Trace *one* section and cut out. Place tracing over squared paper, and rule diagonal lines for diamond pattern, as illustrated.

Cut this piece in coffee felt – adding about 3 mm ($\frac{1}{8}$ in) extra on straight edges. Mark ends of ruled lines on felt: remove pattern, rule pencil lines between marks, then stick metallic braid over lines to form criss-cross pattern.

Stitch felt to centre of interfacing. Stick braid along hem of felt. Join straight edges to form centre back seam – stopping 3 cm (1 in) from the top. Fit on doll and join remainder of seam.

FOUNDATION: Use heavy paper to make the skirt stand out correctly. Draw the pattern exactly as diagram 1 – but *include* the shaded section when cutting out, and cut the waist a little lower. Curve round and pin overlap near the base. Fit on doll, under kirtle, and push well up, pinning overlap again nearer the top. Trim lower edge level.

CUTTING ROSE FELT: Cut the skirt once – allowing extra along straight edges, as kirtle. Cut the sleeve and bodice back twice each, and the front once.

SKIRT: Fit round doll, straight edges meeting at centre front: slip-stitch together for 2 cm ($\frac{3}{4}$ in) below waist. Fold edges of skirt smoothly under to reveal kirtle, as shown, and stitch or stick to hold.

SLEEVES: Oversew side seam between o–x, and turn to right side. Stick braid round lower edge, both outside and inside (see photograph). Gather round top, close to edge, then fit over arm and draw up gathers around top of arm, sleeve centre matching shoulder seam. Stitch neatly to edge of flesh felt all round.

UNDER-SLEEVES: Cut in coffee felt, 6 cm ($2\frac{1}{2}$ in) deep×12 cm ($4\frac{1}{2}$ in) wide. Rule vertical lines 2 cm ($\frac{3}{4}$ in) apart. Right side inside, join short edges to form side seam. Using a gathering thread, stitch lace to overlap lower edge. Turn to right side.

Stick cream braid over lines and seam, to within 3 mm ($\frac{1}{8}$ in) of each edge, cutting braid to a point at wrist end.

Turn sleeve right back, then fit under-sleeve over forearm and draw up tightly round wrist. Separate a face tissue into two layers: lightly crumple

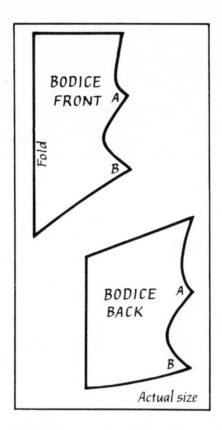

Actual size

one and push down inside to puff out lower half. Gather top edge and draw up round arm at elbow level. Pull sleeve down over top.

BODICE: Oversew side seams (A–B) and turn to right side. Fit round doll, pinning into position. Slip-stitch armhole edges neatly over sleeves, then stitch centre back overlap, and finally the lower edge smoothly over top of skirt.

DECORATION AND JEWELLERY: Stick braids around neck, waistline and skirt, following the illustration.

Use tiny gilt beads, a diamanté or rhinestone, a sequin and tiny pearl, etcetera, to make necklace, chain and pendant, as illustrated: catch at back of neck.

HAIR: Follow directions for the Basic Style (p. 26).

HEADDRESS: Cut the horseshoe shape in thin card, and cover one side with rose felt. Stick folded braid over the cut edge all round, then decorate front with more braid, pearls, etcetera.

Cut the hood in black felt. Join between A–B to form inside centre back seam. Turn to right side. Gather round top, then pin over back of head, drawing up gathers to fit. Catch into place underneath.

Fit horseshoe round head as illustrated: stick and pin sides to hold securely in position.

Titania – Queen of the Fairies

William Shakespeare wrote his play, *A Midsummer Night's Dream*, during the reign of Elizabeth I. There were many similarities between 'Gloriana', as Good Queen Bess was often called, and Shakespeare's fairy queen, Titania. The jewelled dress, butterfly collar and floating cape which Titania wears, are all typical Elizabethan fashions which the Queen herself made popular.

Instructions are given for the skirt decoration as pictured: but you could easily redesign this in any way you please, to incorporate whatever braids and baubles you have available.

MATERIALS: Gold felt, 40 cm×25 cm (16 in×10 in), for dress
Lime green felt, 17 cm×15 cm (7 in×6 in), for skirt panels and shoulders
Lemon yellow felt, 5 cm×8 cm (2 in×3 in), for stomacher and shoulders
Lace, 13 cm×6 cm (5 in×2¼ in), for headdress
Heavy white Vilene or Pellon, 40 cm×25 cm (16 in×10 in), for skirt interfacing and collar
Soft white Vilene or Pellon, 18 cm×10 cm (7 in×4 in), for sleeves
Transparent Vilene or Pellon (or fine net, tulle or chiffon), 30 cm (12 in) square, for cape
Transparent Vilene or Pellon or tissue paper, to back skirt panels
Narrow braids in toning colours to trim – as illustrated:
180 cm (2 yd) creamy yellow, for skirt panels
15 cm (6 in) pale olive green, for shoulders
10 cm (4 in) *very* narrow olive green, for stomacher

45

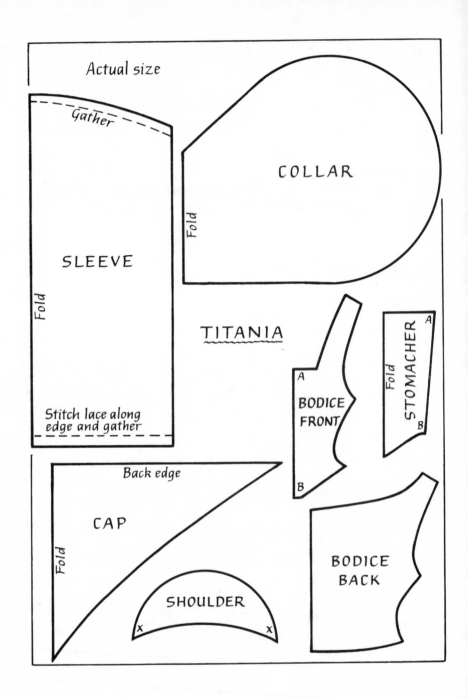

Actual size

Gather

SLEEVE

Fold

Stitch lace along
edge and gather

COLLAR

Fold

TITANIA

A

BODICE
FRONT

B

STOMACHER

Fold

A

B

Back edge

CAP

Fold

SHOULDER

x   x

BODICE
BACK

18 cm (7 in) golden yellow, for neckline
50 cm (20 in) wider golden yellow, for hem
85 cm (1 yd) narrow metallic gold braid, for skirt
Scrap of embroidered trimming for stomacher (optional)
70 cm (¾ yd) very narrow white lace, for sleeves, neck and collar
17 cm (6½ in) narrow white guipure lace, to trim headdress
Amber, diamanté or rhinestones, tiny glass and gilt beads, assorted pearls (including one tear-drop), etcetera, for decoration and jewellery
Cartridge or construction paper for foundation
Double knitting wool or thick-knit yarn for hair
All-purpose clear adhesive (for beads)
Fabric adhesive

SLEEVES: Cut twice in soft Vilene or Pellon.

Join side seam and turn to right side. Gather top edge, then fit on doll, drawing up round top of arm, seam underneath: distribute the gathers evenly, but with more fullness at the top. Catch edge of flesh felt over top of sleeve.

Stitch narrow lace around lower edge with a gathering thread, and draw up tightly round wrist.

SKIRT PATTERN: Follow directions for The Real Princess (p. 41).

SKIRT: Cut first in heavy interfacing. Rule a pencil line to mark the centre (D–E on diagram 1): then rule lines dividing each half into three, as shown. Pin this piece to the back of your felt, and cut level. Tack (baste) along each marked line.

Right side inside, join straight edges of skirt felt to form centre back seam – stopping 3 cm (1¼ in) from the top. Join the interlining in the same way. Turn to right side and fit on doll: make sure interlining is flat, then slip-stitch remainder of seam.

FOUNDATION: Follow directions for The Real Princess (p. 42).

SHOULDERS: Cut twice in lime. Stick each piece to lemon felt and cut level. Stick narrow braid round outer edge of lime sides, then fit round

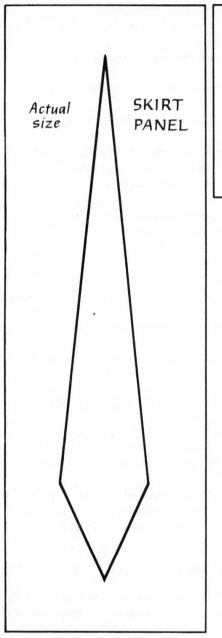

Actual size

SKIRT PANEL

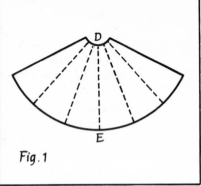

Fig.1

opposite: Titania
following page: Little Miss Muffet

top of arm, over sleeves, and catch corners x–x with a long thread underneath: catch to flesh felt at top.

BODICE: Cut the front and back twice each in gold, and the stomacher once in lemon.

Right sides together, oversew stomacher between the two bodice fronts, matching A–B. Join to back pieces at sides and shoulders. Turn to right side. Stick lace inside neckline.

Fit bodice on doll, easing armholes gently over shoulders. Pin smoothly, overlapping at centre back and over top of skirt, then slip-stitch centre back, and round armholes and waist.

SKIRT DECORATION: Trace the panel six times on transparent interfacing or tissue paper. Stick to back of lime felt: when dry, cut out. Stick braid round edge and decorate with diamanté or rhinestones surrounded by tiny beads – or a similar motif. Stick five panels to skirt, centred over tacked or basted lines, tops level with lower edge of bodice. Stick last panel over back seam.

Stick shorter lengths of gold braid between panels and round lower edge of *bodice* only.

Stick wider braid round hem.

BODICE DECORATION: Stick embroidery or lace motif to stomacher, with very narrow braid along sides and lower edge. Stick braid round neckline. Stitch loops of tiny pearls across front, as shown.

HAIR: Follow directions for the Basic Style (p. 26).

JEWELLERY: Thread a necklace of tiny beads, and catch at back of neck. Stitch ear-rings of graduated pearls at sides of face, as illustrated.

CAP: Cut in lace (if possible using finished edge of lace for straight back edge – if not, turn edge under or trim with narrow lace).

Stitch guipure lace along both curved sides, adding pearls, etcetera, if liked. Stitch tear-drop pearl to centre front point.

Fit over top of head and catch into position.

49

CAPE: Gather one edge of square and pin across back between shoulders, following curved neckline of dress. Draw up, distributing gathers evenly, and stitch into place.

COLLAR: Cut in stiff Vilene or Pellon. Edge with narrow lace.

Stitch lower edge across back, following neckline, over gathered edge of cape.

Little Miss Muffet

The early colonists in America must have had to endure unbelievable hardships. But history doesn't tell us whether these included encounters with giant spiders, if they happened to sit on a tuffet to eat their curds and whey! Miss Muffet's attractive dress is based on one originally worn by an American settler in the late 1600s.

Make the standard doll *with wrists* (section 4a, p. 21).

MATERIALS: Dark brown felt, 30 cm (12 in) square, for dress
Leaf green felt, 18 cm × 12 cm (7 in × 5 in), for underskirt, etcetera
White felt, 10 cm × 7 cm (4 in × 3 in), for collar
Soft white Vilene or Pellon, 18 cm × 40 cm (7 in × 16 in), for underskirt and sleeves
20 cm (8 in) narrow white lace
Thick black soft embroidery cotton or crochet yarn or fine cord
Sequin and bead, or alternative, to trim neck
Pearls, beads, flowers, etcetera, for hair (optional)
Double knitting wool or thick-knit yarn for hair
All-purpose clear adhesive (for beads)
Fabric adhesive

UNDERSKIRT: Use the kirtle pattern for The Real Princess (p. 41) to cut the front in green felt. Cut the remainder in Vilene or Pellon, 20 cm (8 in) wide × 17 cm (6¾ in) deep.

Join the straight side edges of the felt piece between the short side edges of the Vilene or Pellon rectangle, *beginning at the bottom:* trim away excess felt at the top.

Gather round top, marking centre back. Fit on doll, draw up gathers evenly round the waist, and secure.

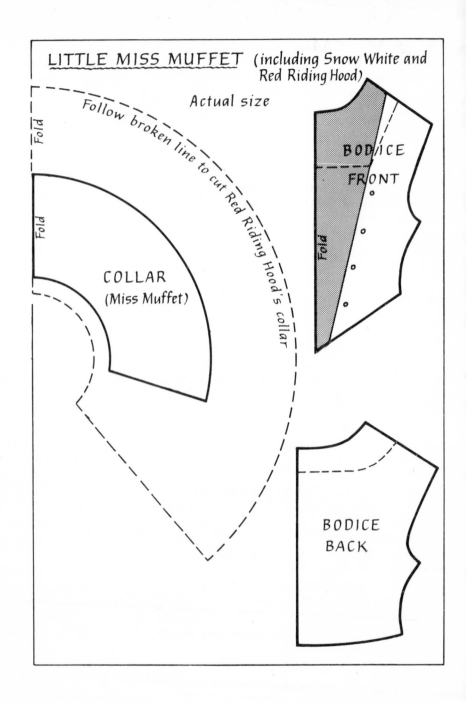

LITTLE MISS MUFFET (including Snow White and Red Riding Hood)

Actual size

Follow broken line to cut Red Riding Hood's collar

Fold

Fold

Fold

COLLAR
(Miss Muffet)

BODICE FRONT

Fold

BODICE BACK

CUTTING BROWN FELT: Cut the skirt 30 cm (12 in) wide × 17 cm (6¾ in) deep. Cut the bodice front once, and the back twice. Cut the sleeve twice – using the pattern for Titania's sleeve (p. 46), but making it 2.5 cm (1 in) shorter.

SKIRT: Gather along the top edge, then draw up tightly round the waist, corners meeting at centre front. Catch lower corners to underskirt.

UNDER-SLEEVES: Use the pattern for Titania's sleeve (p. 46) – but make it 1 cm (⅜ in) shorter. Cut twice in soft Vilene or Pellon.

Join the side seam. Gather round lower edge. Without turning to the right side, fit over arm, lower edge of sleeve level with top of wrist, and rest of sleeve hanging down over hand. Draw up gathers round wrist, and secure.

Gather round top of sleeve, then pull it up the arm, turning it to the right side as you do so. Draw up gathers tightly and evenly round top of arm.

BODICE: Trace a separate pattern for the shaded centre front section, following the straight lines on the pattern for side edges. Place this tracing centrally on the brown felt bodice front, and cut the felt level with the sides. Pin this piece of felt to your green felt, and use it as a pattern to cut the front section – but add about 3 mm (⅛ in) extra at each side.

Keeping the two pieces pinned together, lightly stick the side pieces of the bodice to the overlapping edges of the green centre – carefully matching the brown sides and centre edge-to-edge. Remove the brown centre section, then slip-stitch bodice sides to green centre.

Criss-cross black embroidery or crochet cotton, etcetera, between o's to form front lacing, as illustrated.

Right sides together, join the front to the back pieces along side and shoulder seams. Turn to the right side. Fit on doll, pinning into position over skirt gathers, and overlapping edges of centre back opening: then slip-stitch into place.

DRESS SLEEVES: Join side seam and turn to right side. Gather round top.

Now cut a slit straight up the *front* of the sleeve, parallel with the side seam, but 2 cm (¾ in) away from it – beginning at the lower edge and ending 2 cm (¾ in) below the top edge (see diagram). Catch slit edges together 1 cm (⅜ in) above lower edge of sleeve, as indicated: then turn up to form cuff.

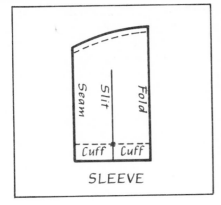

SLEEVE

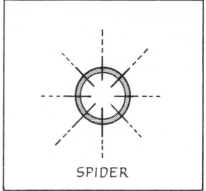

SPIDER

Fit sleeve over arm and draw up evenly round top, over the under-sleeve: then catch edge of bodice neatly over gathers all round.

Make second sleeve in the same way – but remember to reverse position of slash.

COLLAR: Cut in white felt (ignore broken line). Stitch lace round outer edge. Fit around neck and catch top corners together at centre front. Trim with a sequin and bead or alternative 'brooch'.

HAIR: Make tied skeins as directed for styled hair on p. 25.

1. Wind wool twenty times around a 14-cm (5½-in) deep card: tie sides tightly, and centre fairly tightly. Stick across top of head, over seam: catch ends down securely.

2. Wind wool fifteen times around a 13-cm (5-in) deep card: tie sides and centre tightly. Fold in half and stick centre immediately behind last piece, bringing ends down and spreading out to cover back of head, catching neatly into place.

3. Wind wool ten times around an 8-cm (3-in) deep card: tie as first skein. Stick across back of head at nape of neck, covering ends of previous piece: take ends up to seam to meet ends of first skein, and catch into place.

4. Wind wool twenty times around a 19-cm (7½-in) deep card: tie as first skein. Stick in front of first skein, taking the ends down over the face as illustrated, then curving them up over the two previous ends at each side, and catching them into place there.

5. Make a bunch of loops for loose hair (p. 25). Wind wool ten times

around a 13-cm (5-in) deep card. Stitch to crown of head, to hang down back of head. Cut loops.

6. Make another tied skein, winding wool fifteen times around a 19-cm (7½-in) deep card: tie sides tightly, but not centre. Twist into a loose knot, tucking the ends away neatly underneath. Stick to crown of head, using plenty of adhesive.

Trim bun with pearls or beads, and flowers, as illustrated – or leave undecorated.

Miss Muffet's Spider

MATERIALS: Brown felt for body
Three pipe cleaners
Sequins and glass-headed pins or beads, for eyes
Kapok, polyester fiberfill or alternative, to stuff
Harbutt's Plasticine or modelling clay
Stiff card
Brown ink, marker or paint
Fabric adhesive

BASE: Cut a 2.5-cm (1-in) diameter circle of card and stick to felt. Cut felt fractionally larger.

LEGS: Cut eight 5-cm (2-in) lengths of pipe cleaner and colour them with ink or paint. When dry, stick to the card as diagram, each extending 4 cm (1½ in) beyond edge of felt. Roll a small ball of Plasticine and press down on top of card.

BODY: Cut a 5-cm (2-in) diameter circle of felt, and gather neatly round the edge. Mark the edge into quarters, then draw up to fit the smaller circle: place a little stuffing in centre, then fit over Plasticine, and pin between legs, distributing the gathers evenly. Oversew edges neatly together.

FINISHING: Bend legs up, and position eyes, as illustrated.

55

Snow White

The story of Snow White and the Seven Dwarfs is perhaps even more popular than the other fairytale which the Brothers Grimm wrote, about her adventures with her sister, Rose Red. Whichever is your favourite, here is a charming outfit, both practical and pretty, which emphasises her gentle personality. This is an example of how you can adapt one set of patterns to make a costume which, at first glance, looks quite different. Now take a second look – and compare Snow White with Miss Muffet . . .

MATERIALS: Red felt, 25 cm×35 cm (10 in×14 in), for dress
Grey felt, 10 cm×20 cm (4 in×8 in), for sleeves and bodice
Olive green felt, 12 cm×7 cm (4¾ in×2¾ in), for apron
Medium-weight black (or white) Vilene or Pellon, 30 cm (12 in) wide by 17 cm (6¾ in) deep, for petticoat
40 cm (½ yd) very narrow toning braid, for dress
18 cm (7 in) narrow black lace, for sleeve frills
35 cm (14 in) narrow black lace, to edge apron
Scraps of white lace and black braid, for bodice
Scraps of embroidered ribbon, narrow lace, etcetera, to trim apron
30 cm (12 in) white lace, to edge petticoat
Thick black soft embroidery cotton or crochet yarn or fine cord
Double knitting wool or thick-knit yarn for hair
Raffia, two pipe cleaners and artificial flowers (optional), for basket
Fabric adhesive

PETTICOAT: Join the two short edges to form centre back seam, and turn to right side. Sew lace round hem. Gather top edge: mark sides and centre

56

front. Fit on doll and draw up tightly just below the natural waistline: distribute gathers evenly all round, and secure thread.

CUTTING RED FELT: Cut the skirt 35 cm (14 in) wide×17 cm (6¾ in) deep. Cut the bodice front once and the back twice, using the pattern for Little Miss Muffet (p. 52), but *following broken line for neck.*

SKIRT: Make up as petticoat, ignoring lace. Then draw·up round waist, just above top of petticoat.

APRON: Trim with bands of ribbon,. lace, etcetera, as illustrated, then sew lace round outer edge.

Gather top edge. Pin top corners at sides of waist, draw up over front of skirt and catch securely into place.

SLEEVES: Using grey felt, make and fit as directed for Titania's sleeve (p. 46).

BODICE: Follow the directions for Little Miss Muffet (p. 53), using grey felt for the centre front section. Then trim the top edge with lace and braid, as illustrated, and stick braid along the front and neck edges, and round armholes.

HAIR: Follow the directions for the Basic Style (p. 26).

Finally, wind wool twenty times around an 8-cm (3-in) deep card: tie sides tightly, but not centre. Stick low across back of head, covering ends of previous two skeins, and catching the ends against the side seam, just below second (front) skein.

BASKET: Use raffia *double.* Tie a knot at one end, then wrap the raffia closely round the knot in a flat circle – oversewing neatly with matching thread. Continue to wind the raffia round, oversewing it to the strand beneath: take care to keep absolutely flat. When the circle is 9 cm (3½ in) in diameter, finish off neatly.

Place the two pipe cleaners side-by-side and bind tightly with double raffia, for the handle: stick raffia at ends. Bend circle up to form basket, as illustrated: then curve handle round and stitch to sides and underneath.

Red Riding Hood

Snow White becomes Red Riding Hood when she puts on this romantic cape, which is copied from one worn by another, later, American colonist, in the eighteenth century. The original must have been cosy enough to withstand the hardest winter, because it was completely fur-lined – and had a giant fur muff trimmed with ribbon bow-knots to match the cape.

MATERIALS: Red felt, 20 cm×90 cm (8 in×36 in) *OR* two 22-cm (9-in) squares, one 20-cm (8-in) square and one 15-cm (6-in) square
45 cm ($\frac{1}{2}$ yd) lambswool trimming
25 cm ($\frac{1}{4}$ yd) very narrow dark brown satin ribbon
Tiny hook and eye
10 cm (4 in) black lace, 1.5 cm ($\frac{3}{8}$ in) deep, for ᴍittens (optional)
Brown raffia for basket
Fabric adhesive

Cut a piece 44 cm (17$\frac{1}{2}$ in) deep×20 cm (8 in) wide, for the cape or join two pieces 22 cm×20 cm (8$\frac{3}{4}$ in×8 in). Following diagram 1, cut a 2-cm ($\frac{3}{4}$-in) diameter circle exactly in the centre, for the neck: then cut straight up from lower edge, as indicated, for centre front opening.

For hood pattern, draw a 20-cm (8-in) diameter semi-circle, extending it below broken line, as diagram 3.

Cut the collar as Miss Muffet (p. 52) – but *follow the broken line.*

CAPE: Right side inside, fold in half as broken line, diagram 1. Mark point A at each side, 4 cm (1$\frac{1}{2}$ in) below fold (diagram 2). Oversew side edges together between A–B.

HOOD: Gather all round upper edge, from corner to corner as indicated, but don't draw up. Then gather lower edge and pin around inner edge of

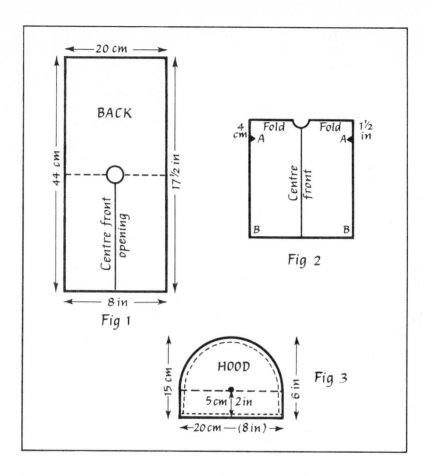

Fig 1

20 cm — BACK — 44 cm — 17½ in — Centre front opening — 8 in

Fig 2

4 cm — Fold — A — Centre front — Fold — A — 1½ in — B — B

Fig 3

HOOD — 15 cm — 6 in — 5 cm — 2 in — 20 cm — (8 in)

collar, right sides together and centres matching. Draw up gathers to fit, distributing evenly, and stitch.

COLLAR: Pin hood and collar round neck edge of cape, wrong sides of hood and cape together, centres matching as before. Oversew securely all round, then turn to right side. Catch edges of collar to cape at centre front. Stitch hook and eye at neck opening.

FINISHING HOOD: Fit cape on doll, with hood over head. Draw up gathers to fit snugly round face, and secure: distribute evenly, but with more fullness round upper half. Remove carefully and stick lambswool edging over gathers. Edge cuffs in the same way (trim lambswool to length either before or after applying, as preferred).

BOW-KNOTS: Make tiny bows of folded ribbon, bound tightly with matching thread at the centre. Fold a short length of ribbon in half, catch fold behind centre of bow and trim ends, for ties. Stitch to hood and neck as illustrated.

MITTENS: Catch lace around hand, oversewing cut edges neatly inside palm.

BASKET: Follow the directions to begin Snow White's basket (p. 57): but when the flat circle measures 3 cm (1¼ in) in diameter, oversew the next round at an angle – and continue shaping the sides in this direction. When the basket is about 4 cm (1½ in) deep, turn again for the top edge, then finish off neatly.

Twist several strands of raffia for the handle: curve over, and sew the ends inside the basket. (Or make a handle with pipe cleaners, as for Snow White.)

Cinderella

Ragged and lonely, Cinderella's charm lies in her shy lack of sophistication. Emphasise this quality in the colours you choose for her dress. The total effect must be dull – almost drab – but that doesn't prevent it being attractive, too. Experiment with different colour schemes, combining softly muted shades like nut brown/mid-olive/harvest gold, or russet/ stone/pale grey, or pale blue/lavender/mid-grey.

Make the basic figure *with wrists* (section 4a – p. 21).

MATERIALS: Lilac felt, 25 cm×20 cm (10 in×8 in), for dress
Rose felt, 16 cm×20 cm (6½ in×8 in), for dress
Grey felt, 33 cm×25 cm (13 in×10 in), for underskirt
Black Vilene or Pellon, as above, to line underskirt
Soft (or lightweight) white Vilene or Pellon,
  18 cm×5 cm (7 in×2 in), for fichu
Transparent (or light-weight) Vilene or Pellon for
  cap: a 24-cm (9½-in) diameter circle
20 cm (8 in) narrow ribbon to trim cap
Double knitting wool or thick-knit yarn for hair
Very fine twigs, grass seed heads or raffia, for broom
Thin garden cane or alternative, 12 cm (5 in) long, for
  broomstick
Fabric adhesive

UNDERSKIRT: Make the skirt pattern for The Real Princess (p. 41). Cut in grey felt, using pinking shears for the lower edge. Tack (baste) felt to Vilene or Pellon, keeping stitches 2 cm (¾ in) inside the straight side edges, and cut again.

Right side inside, join straight edges of felt to form centre back seam – stopping 3 cm (1¼ in) from the top. Join the lining in the same way. Turn to right side and fit on doll: make sure lining is flat, then slip-stitch remainder of seam.

61

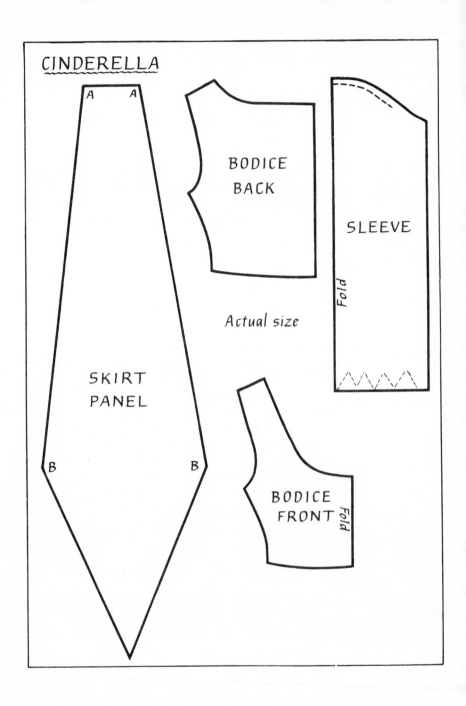

CINDERELLA

A A

BODICE
BACK

SLEEVE

Fold

Actual size

SKIRT
PANEL

B   B

BODICE
FRONT

Fold

CUTTING THE DRESS FELTS: In lilac, cut the bodice front once, the back and sleeve twice each, and the skirt panel four times. Cut the skirt panel four times more in rose.

OVERSKIRT: Right sides together, oversew the panels together alternately, between A–B: then join the last to the first, leaving 3 cm (1¼ in) open at the top. Turn to right side and gather top edge.

Fit on doll. Slip-stitch opening (at back), then draw up gathers tightly, distributing them evenly around the waist.

SLEEVES: Join side seam and turn to right side. Cut inverted V-shapes round lower edge for ragged effect. Gather round top, then fit on doll. Draw up and catch top edge to flesh felt all round.

BODICE: Join front to back pieces along side and shoulder seams. Turn to right side. Fit on doll, pinning the back overlap and waist. Slip-stitch armholes over tops of sleeves: then slip-stitch centre back opening, and catch lower edge over skirt gathers.

FICHU: Drape round the neck as illustrated, folding into tiny pleats and then tucking the ends smoothly down inside the bodice front.

HAIR: Make a skein of wool as directed for loose hair (p. 25), winding wool or yarn twenty times around a 20-cm (8-in) deep card. Now tie the skein, quite loosely, 4 cm (1½ in) from the tied end: remove first tie and cut loops at this end. Stick over top of head, spreading tied section across seam, so that the cut ends cover the forehead, and the loops hang down the back. Catch securely to head.

Wind wool twenty times around a 30-cm (12-in) deep card. Slide off carefully and tie fairly loosely at the centre. Stick across top and sides of head, spreading out evenly.

Cut loops and trim ends.

CAP: Mark a 16-cm (6½-in) diameter circle inside your 24-cm (9½-in) diameter circle. Gather along this line, then draw up evenly round head, as illustrated, catching at front and back.

Make a ribbon bow and stitch at centre front.

BROOM: Bind twigs, grass heads, raffia, etcetera, around end of stick – using raffia or brown thread.

Mary-Mary, Quite Contrary

How does your garden grow?
With silver bells and cockle shells,
And pretty maids all in a row.

In 1682 William Penn took his family from England to America, where he set up a Quaker colony, and founded Pennsylvania.

Mary-Mary's dress is based on a typical Quaker costume of the late eighteenth century, with a white fichu knotted at the back, and a green apron. But at that time the traditional bonnet, although similar in shape to this one, had a narrower brim – so that it formed a close-fitting cap. Mary-Mary's flattering, deep-brimmed version was all the rage in Philadelphia around 1812!

MATERIALS: Brown felt, 40 cm×25 cm (16 in×10 in), for dress
Camel felt, 35 cm (14 in) wide ×17 cm (6¾ in) deep, for underskirt
Green felt, 8 cm (3 in) wide×12 cm (4¾ in) deep, for apron
Black felt, 10 cm (4 in) square, for boots
Stiff white Vilene or Pellon, 25 cm (10 in) wide×16 cm (6¼ in) deep, for petticoat: 5 cm×10 cm (2 in×4 in), for cuffs: 18 cm (7 in) square, for bonnet (or use white felt)
Soft white Vilene or Pellon, 28 cm×11 cm (11 in×4½ in), for fichu: a 15-cm (6-in) diameter circle for bonnet (or use white felt)
Thin white card or hat buckram to stiffen bonnet brim
35 cm (14 in) brown braid to trim underskirt
25 cm (¼ yd) very narrow white ribbon for bonnet strings

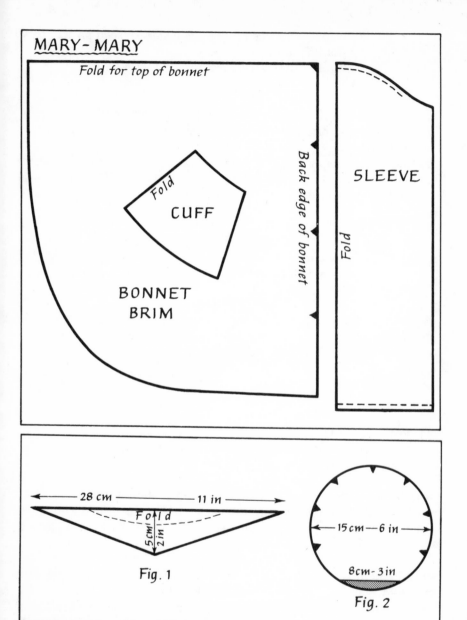

MARY-MARY

Fold for top of bonnet

Fold

CUFF

BONNET
BRIM

Back edge of bonnet

SLEEVE

Fold

28 cm —— 11 in

Fold

5 cm
2 in

Fig. 1

15 cm — 6 in

8 cm - 3 in

Fig. 2

opposite: Mother Hubbard
previous page: Mary-Mary, Quite Contrary

Twelve to fourteen tiny black beads (or seed pearls)
for boot buttons
Double knitting wool or thick-knit yarn for hair
Fabric adhesive

BOOTS: Follow the directions on p. 23, using black felt for the whole foot, and stitching tiny black beads down the side of each boot.

PETTICOAT: Overlap and join the side edges to form centre back seam. Gather round top, fit on doll and draw up about 1 cm below the natural waistline: distribute the gathers evenly, and secure to body to hold in place.

UNDERSKIRT: Join side edges and turn to right side. Sew or stick trimming round hem. Gather top edge, mark sides and centre, then fit on doll and draw up evenly just below the natural waistline: catch to body as before.

CUTTING THE BROWN FELT: Cut a piece 40 cm (16 in) wide by 15.5 cm (6 in) deep, for the skirt. Cut the sleeve twice. Use the patterns for Cinderella's bodice (p. 62): cut the front once and back twice.

SKIRT: Make and fit as underskirt, omitting trimming, and positioning at waist level.

SLEEVES: Join side seam, and turn to right side. Gather round top and fit on doll: draw up and catch top edge to flesh felt all round. Gather lower edge and draw up tightly round wrist.

BODICE: Join front to back pieces along side and shoulder seams. Turn to right side. Fit on doll, pinning the back overlap and waist. Slip-stitch armholes over tops of sleeves: then slip-stitch centre back opening, and catch lower edge over skirt gathers.

FICHU: Cut in folded Vilene or Pellon, as shown in figure 1. Retaining first fold, fold again, in a gentle curve as broken line: wrap around the neck and shoulders, the first folded edge inside, and the second fold finding its natural line as you cross the triangle over at the front and take the ends round under the arms. Catch together at centre back of waist.

CUFFS: Cut in stiff Vilene or Pellon. Fit around wrists, as illustrated, overlap side edge and join over sleeve seams.

APRON: Gather top edge and draw up to measure about 5 cm (2 in). Stitch across front of waist.

HAIR: Follow the directions for stage 1 of the Basic Style (p. 26).
Then wind the wool tightly around the tip of your forefinger five times: catch the loops together with matching thread. Without cutting wool or thread, make an identical set of loops alongside. Stitch the pair of loops just below the base of the first skein of hair – alongside the seam, but on the front half of the head, and facing forward. Repeat at other side.
Continue with remaining stages of Basic Style, looping the ends of the second skein over the back of the bunches of loops, so that they appear from underneath.

BONNET: Cut the brim in card or buckram. Stick lightly to stiff Vilene or Pellon, then cut this 2–3 mm (⅛ in) larger all round. Stick Vilene or Pellon to other side of card and cut again – level with edge of first side. Oversew sides and front edge neatly. Mark the back edge into eight equal sections.
Cut a 15-cm (6-in) diameter circle of soft Vilene or Pellon for the back: draw an 8-cm (3-in) line across the base, for lower edge, as figure 2, and cut away shaded section below. Mark the edge at centre top, then mark each side equally into four, as indicated. Gather all round curved edge.
With right sides together, oversew the back edge of the brim round the gathered edge of the back, matching marked points and distributing gathers evenly between. Ease bonnet gently over to right side.
Gather lower edge and draw up across back of neck.
Stitch ribbon strings inside brim: fit on doll and tie under chin.

Lucy Locket, Lost her Pocket. . . .

Down the centuries, France had gradually become the accepted leader of the fashion world. Ladies on both sides of the Atlantic looked to Paris when choosing the latest styles for their wardrobe. Then, at the beginning of the eighteenth century, Paris fashions suddenly became extremely slim and close-fitting. Dresses were of clinging materials, so fine you could see right through them. But the ladies of England and America were more modest than the French – and preferred to keep warm, too! They copied the high waistline and narrow skirt from France, but in fabrics which made their dresses demure and pretty: like Lucy Locket's outfit, with a flattering bonnet and dainty purse to match.

MATERIALS: Olive green felt, 22 cm (9 in) square, for dress, and
        25 cm×10 cm (10 in×4 in), for bonnet
Lilac felt, 13 cm×27 cm (5 in×10½ in), for yoke,
        sleeves and stockings, and 20 cm×10 cm
        (8 in×4 in), for bonnet
Plum (or lilac) felt, 6 cm×4 cm (2 in×1½ in), for purse
Black felt for shoes
Soft white Vilene or Pellon (or felt), 15 cm×5 cm
        (6 in×2 in), for pantalettes
Heavy Vilene or Pellon, or hat buckram or thin card,
        25 cm×10 cm (10 in×4 in), to stiffen bonnet
15 cm (6 in) narrow broderie anglaise or eyelet
        embroidery
70 cm (¾ yd) very narrow white lace
70 cm (¾ yd) very narrow lilac ribbon
50 cm (½ yd) lilac ribbon, 1–1.5 cm (½ in) wide, for sash
25 cm (10 in) embroidered trimming for skirt
70 cm (¾ yd) narrow olive braid for skirt (optional)
        and bonnet

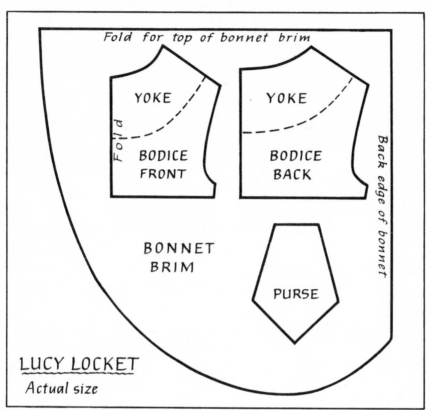

Fold for top of bonnet brim

Fold

YOKE

YOKE

BODICE FRONT

BODICE BACK

Back edge of bonnet

BONNET BRIM

PURSE

LUCY LOCKET

Actual size

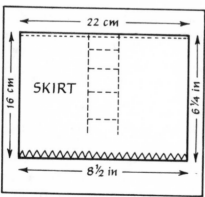

22 cm

16 cm

SKIRT

6¼ in

8½ in

35 cm (14 in) white silk braid for bonnet
Artificial flowers to trim bonnet
Gold gift-tie or fine chain, tiny gilt beads, stranded
   embroidery cotton, and embroidered trim, for
   purse
Thick black soft embroidery cotton or crochet yarn
   for shoestrings
Double knitting wool or thick-knit yarn for hair
Fabric adhesive

FEET: Make up in lilac felt, with 1-cm ($\frac{3}{8}$-in) wide strips of black felt for the shoes, as directed on p. 16. Finally, thread shoestring through front of foot, between top edges of shoe, as illustrated: cross ends in front, take round to back and tie neatly behind ankle.

PANTALETTES: Cut two pieces of Vilene or Pellon, 5 cm (2 in) deep×7.5 cm (3 in) wide. Stitch edging along bottom of each, then fit round legs and join side edges to form centre back seams. Catch top round leg so that edging is at ankle level.

CUTTING THE DRESS FELTS: Cut the skirt in olive felt, 22 cm (8$\frac{1}{2}$ in) wide×16 cm (6$\frac{1}{4}$ in) deep (see diagram): cut the bodice front once and the back twice. Cut the pattern for Titania's sleeve (p. 46) twice in lilac. Trace separate patterns for the yoke, following broken lines on bodice front and back: cut front once and back twice, in lilac.

SKIRT: Cut a jagged lower edge, as indicated, each point 1 cm ($\frac{3}{8}$ in) deep×1 cm ($\frac{3}{8}$ in) wide. Stick or sew lace, braid and embroidered trimming for centre front panel, following the illustration and diagram for guidance: mark the vertical lines 4 cm (1$\frac{1}{2}$ in) apart, with the first horizontal bar 2 cm ($\frac{3}{4}$ in) from the top, increasing the distance between the lower bars by 5 mm ($\frac{1}{4}$ in) each time.

Join side edges to form centre back seam, and turn to right side. Gather top edge, mark sides and fit on doll: draw up evenly round body, close under arms, and catch to lower edge of flesh felt all round.

SLEEVES: Mark each side edge 1.5 cm ($\frac{5}{8}$ in) below the top: draw a line across the sleeve between these points.

Join side seam and turn to the right side. Gather top edge, and also along marked line. Fit on doll, drawing up top gathers around top of arm: distribute gathers evenly, but with more fullness at the top, and catch over edge of flesh felt all round.

Draw up lower gathers tightly round arm, to form puff sleeve. Then stitch lace round lower edge and draw up tightly round wrist. Bind sleeve neatly at these two points with narrow ribbon, as shown.

BODICE: Tack (baste) yoke to front and back pieces, then appliqué lower edges to bodice.

Right sides together, join front to back pieces along shoulder seams. Turn to right side. Stitch gathered lace round lower edge of yoke, and also round neck to form a tiny stand-up collar.

Fit on doll and pin centre back overlap. Join sides under arms, then slip-stitch armholes neatly over sleeve gathers. Slip-stitch centre back opening and catch lower edge over top of skirt.

Tie sash around waist, making a large bow at the back, and trimming ribbon ends neatly.

HAIR: Follow directions for stage 1 of the Basic Style (p. 26).

Now wind wool ten times around the tip of your forefinger: catch loops together at one side. Make a second bunch of loops in the same way. Stitch these side-by-side to the forehead, 1 cm (⅜ in) in front of the centre of the skein.

Complete the remaining stages of the Basic Style, positioning the second skein between skein 1 and the loops.

BONNET: Cut brim once in each felt, and again in stiffening. Cut a 6-cm (2⅜-in) diameter circle once each in olive felt and stiffening, for the back.

Tack (baste) the brim stiffening between the two felt pieces, then oversew all round the curved edge. Tack (baste) the two back pieces together, then oversew the straight edge of the brim round the back: oversew neatly round remainder of back.

Stick white braid inside edge of brim, and olive braid outside and round back. Catch the centre of a 50-cm (18-in) length of ribbon to top of bonnet, close to back, then sew flowers on top.

Fit on doll, pin if necessary, and tie at side of face, as illustrated.

PURSE: Cut twice in felt.

Wind embroidery cotton six to eight times around the tip of your finger:

pass a strand of cotton through the loops and tie tightly – then bind the loops, close under first tie, to form head of tassel. Cut lower loops neatly.

Oversew felt together round sides and base, catching in tassel at base, and also the ends of a 5-cm (2-in) length of gift-tie, chain, etcetera, at top corners, for handle.

Stitch beads at centre top, and stick trimming to front.

Old Mother Hubbard

In the nineteenth century, married and elderly ladies wore dainty lace caps indoors: they smothered them with all manner of ribbons, frills, flowers and bows – the more the merrier – and thought them incredibly smart.

Perhaps Old Mother Hubbard spent all her money trimming her new cap to the heights of fashion . . . and that's why the cupboard was bare when she went there to get her poor dog a bone!

MATERIALS: Blue felt, 35 cm×30 cm (14 in×20 in), for dress
Gold felt, 30 cm (12 in) wide by 17 cm (6¾ in) deep, for underskirt
Vilene or Pellon, as above, for underskirt lining
1 metre (1⅛ yd) narrow greenish-gold braid to decorate skirt
120 cm (1⅜ yd) pale blue lace daisies to decorate skirt and cap
30 cm (12 in) gold braid to edge underskirt
35 cm (14 in) heavy cream lace to edge skirt
60 cm (23 in) cream lace, 3 cm (1¼ in) deep, for apron and cap
50 cm (⅝ yd) narrow cream lace for collar, cuffs and apron
40 cm (½ yd) narrow cream ribbon for apron
40 cm (½ yd) narrow blue ribbon for cap
Tiny blue flowers to trim cap
Tiny beads and diamanté or rhinestone, for buttons and brooch
Two brass curtain rings, 2 cm (¾ in) diameter, for spectacles
Grey double knitting wool or thick-knit yarn for hair

73

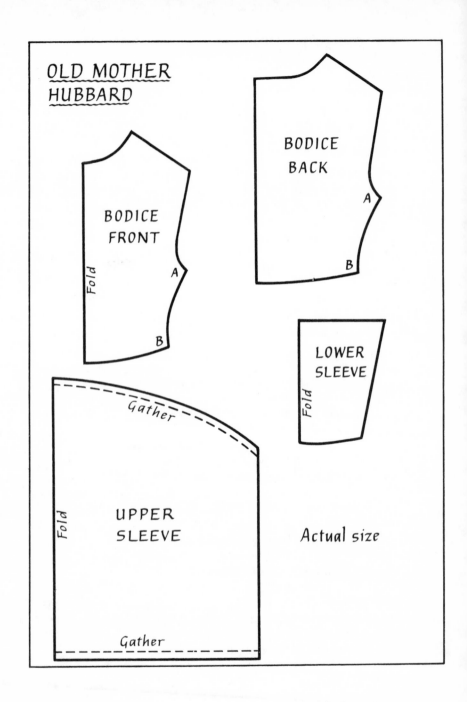

OLD MOTHER
HUBBARD

BODICE
BACK

A

B

BODICE
FRONT

Fold

A

B

LOWER
SLEEVE

Fold

Gather

Fold

UPPER
SLEEVE

Actual size

Gather

All-purpose clear adhesive (for beads)
Fabric adhesive

UNDERSKIRT: Join the short edges of the felt to form centre back seam, and turn to right side. Repeat with lining: then fit inside felt, top edges level and seams matching: gather together round top. Stick gold braid round lower edge of felt.

Mark sides and centre front, then fit on doll and draw up tightly *just below* the natural waistline, distributing the gathers evenly.

CUTTING BLUE FELT: Cut the skirt 35 cm (14 in) wide by 14 cm (5½ in) deep. Cut the bodice front once, the back twice, and the upper and lower sleeves twice each.

SKIRT: Mark vertical lines 2.5 cm (1 in) apart, then stick alternate rows of braid, lace, etcetera, to form stripes. Stick heavy lace behind lower edge, to extend below as illustrated.

Gather top edge. Mark sides and centre front, then fit on doll and draw up tightly round waist, distributing the gathers evenly.

SLEEVES: Gather bottom edge of upper sleeve: pin to top edge of lower sleeve, matching sides and centres. Draw up to fit, and oversew together. Stitch gathered lace along bottom edge of lower sleeve.

Join side seam of *upper* sleeve only: turn to right side. Gather round top edge, fit on doll and draw up gathers round top of arm: distribute evenly and catch to edge of flesh felt all round.

Overlap sides of lower section, and slip-stitch neatly.

BODICE: Join front to back pieces along side seams (A–B). Turn to right side. Fit round body, overlapping and pinning centre back opening. Lap front over back on each shoulder, and slip-stitch neatly. Then slip-stitch armholes over sleeve gathers. Slip-stitch centre back, and catch lower edge of bodice neatly over skirt gathers.

Stitch collar of gathered lace around neck, and stick or sew beads, etcetera, down front for brooch and buttons.

APRON: Overlap three 8-cm (3-in) widths of lace, and join, as illustrated. Trim sides with narrow lace. Gather top edge and draw up across front of skirt, catching corners to waist at each side.

Tie ribbon round waist, catching bow at centre back.

HAIR: Follow directions for the Basic Style (p. 26).

Finally, wind wool ten times around a 13-cm (5-in) deep card: tie sides tightly, but not centre. Tie in a knot, then tie ends together underneath, to form a bun. Stick at nape of neck.

CAP: Overlap and join the straight edges of two 18-cm (7-in) lengths of lace – to form a strip just under 6 cm (2½ in) wide. Gather each cut end and draw up tightly. Now gather along the middle of the back strip: fit cap on doll and draw up gathers to fit snugly round back of head.

Stitch flowers at each side, and stick lace daisies over join. Make a tiny bow in the centre of a 15-cm (6-in) length of ribbon: catch under doll's chin, then stitch ends to hair at each side – catching the cap securely down on top. Make another bow at the centre of the remaining ribbon, and stitch to centre back of cap, under frill, to hang down back of head.

SPECTACLES: Follow directions for eyes as usual, but make your stitches slightly shorter. Then catch curtain rings at each side, joining across the centre with a button-holed bar of matching thread.

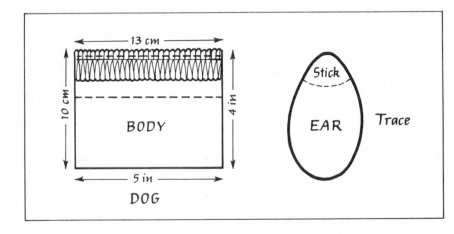

Her Hungry Hound

Lampshade fringe makes a lovely silky dog – but snip strips of felt closely to make your own fringe, if you prefer.

76

MATERIALS: Coffee felt, 15 cm (6 in) square
Dark brown felt, 5 cm × 4 cm (2 in × 1½ in)
Scraps of pink and black felt
1 metre (1 yd) dark brown silk fringe, 2.5 cm (1 in) deep
20 cm (8 in) cream silk fringe, 2.5 cm (1 in) deep
30 cm (12 in) narrow ribbon for neck
Small round black bead for nose (optional)
Pipe cleaner 5 cm (2 in) long
Kapok, polyester fiberfill or alternative stuffing
Stiff card
Harbutt's Plasticine or modelling clay (optional)
Fabric adhesive

CUTTING OUT: In coffee felt, cut a piece as diagram for the body, and a 4-cm (1½-in) diameter circle for the base: cut two 1.4-cm (½-in), and two 1.8-cm (¾-in) diameter circles, for the front and back paws respectively. Cut the ear twice in dark brown. Cut the base again, slightly smaller, in card.

BODY: Pin dark brown fringe along top edge, on right side of felt, as diagram. Stitch, using a gathering thread, but do not draw up.

Mark a horizontal line 4 cm (1½ in) from the top, on the *wrong* side of the felt (broken line on diagram).

Right side inside, join the side edges to form centre back seam. Gather marked line, but don't draw up.

Draw up top gathers as closely as possible, then stitch across top to draw in more tightly. Turn to right side.

TAIL: Wrap a strip of felt round the pipe cleaner, draw in one end neatly, and slip-stitch side edge. Bend at right angles, and fit unfinished end up inside body, securing behind seam.

STUFFING: Half-fill, pushing in firmly, then draw in second row of gathers to form neck. Complete stuffing – adding a ball of Plasticine or alternative, pebble, etcetera, in the centre to weight.

BASE: Stick card to wrong side of felt. Oversew lower edge of body round edge of felt, adding more stuffing before finally closing seam.

77

FRINGE: Stick five 4-cm (1½-in) strips of cream across the front, an equal distance apart, beginning at the bottom and ending at the neck.

Stick lengths of brown round rest of body in the same way.

Roll up a 5-cm (2-in) length of brown, sticking the top edge. Stick firmly, upside-down, to top of head.

EARS: Stick under top-knot at each side of head. Then stick two more rows of fringe to cover back of head, between ears.

PAWS: Stick to front, and *under* base, as illustrated (back lower pair with card).

FACE: Stick or sew bead in centre (or use felt). Cut tiny circles of black felt for his eyes – and a tiny pink tongue. Stick into position.

Where to Buy the Materials for your Storybook Dolls

All the items used were deliberately chosen because they should be easily obtainable, wherever you live. However, if you experience any difficulty, here are my favourite sources of supply.

Coloured felts, wool and yarn, fancy braids and trimmings, lace, ribbon, beads, flowers, stuffing and other craft materials – and all sewing equipment:

John Lewis
Oxford Street, London, W.1.

D. H. Evans
Oxford Street, London, W.1.

The Needlewoman Shop
Regent Street, London, W.1.

Craftsmith
Exeter : Hemel Hempstead : Manchester : Nottingham : Richmond : Slough : Southend.

General craft materials, including coloured felts and stuffing:

Arts and Crafts
10 Byram Street, Huddersfield, Yorks.

Graph paper, greaseproof paper, adhesives, artists' materials and all general stationery:

W. H. Smith and Son Limited.

Sheet foam:

F. W. Woolworth and Company Limited.

U.S.A. Suppliers

Send a self-addressed, stamped envelope to the following major craft suppliers for materials or for the name of the dealer nearest you:

Hazel Pearson Handicrafts,
4128 Temple City Boulevard,
Rosemead, Calif. 91770.

Sondra Schmitz, Sales Manager,
Mangelsen & Sons, Inc.,
8200 J Street,
Omaha, Nebraska 68127.

Susan Davis,
Zim's Inc.,
P.O. Box 7620,
Salt Lake City, Utah 84107.

Crafts Dept. Manager,
Pearl Paint Co., Inc.,
308 Canal Street,
New York, New York 10013.

Mail Order Dept.,
Polk's Hobbies, Inc.,
314 Fifth Avenue,
New York, New York 10001.

There are a number of chains of craft and hobby stores with branches around the U.S.A., including American Handicraft Co., and LeeWards Creative Crafts Centers.